A FIREWALL FOR MIND

SUBHAS BOSE

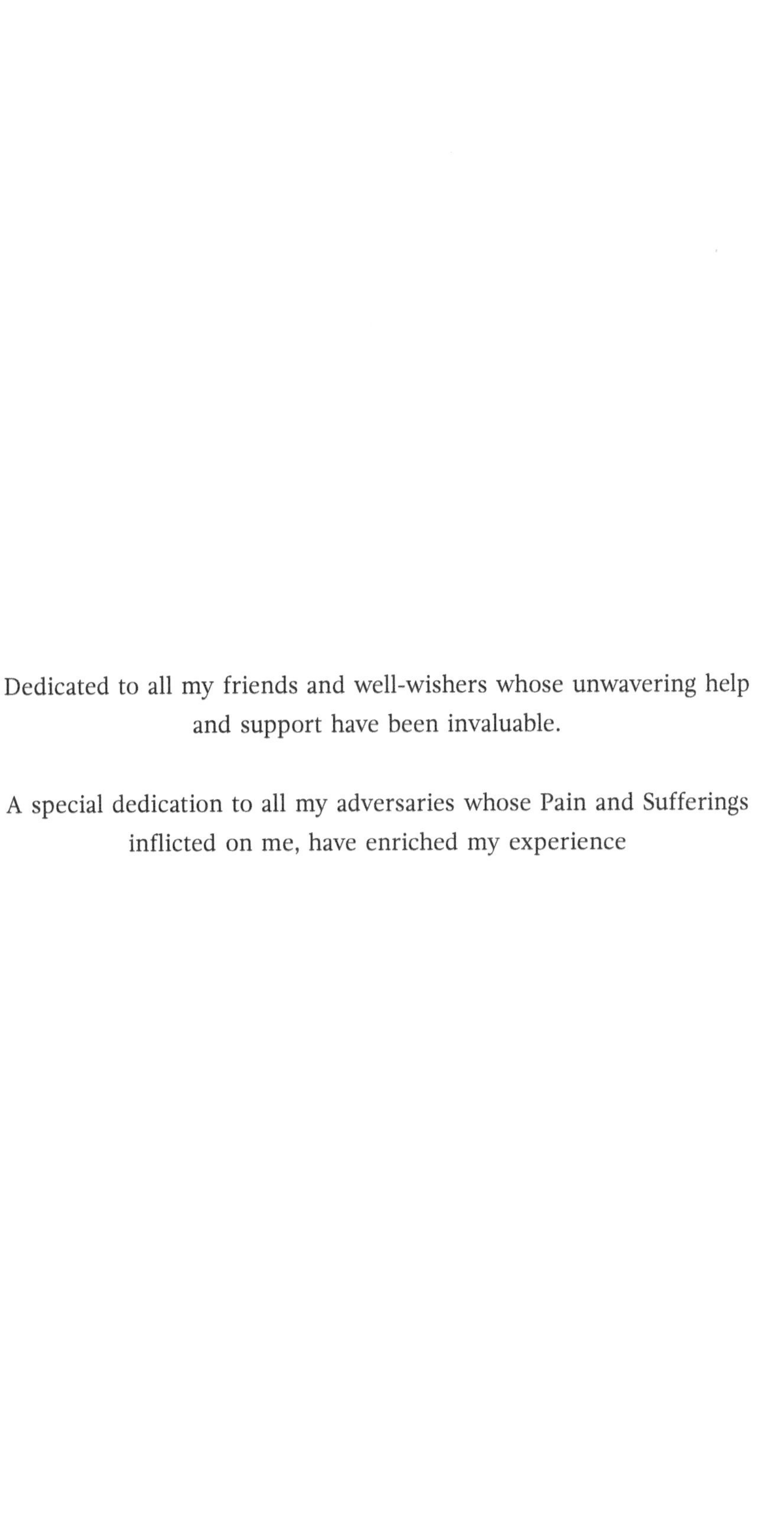

Dedicated to all my friends and well-wishers whose unwavering help and support have been invaluable.

A special dedication to all my adversaries whose Pain and Sufferings inflicted on me, have enriched my experience

Contents

CHAPTER ONE

OUR MIND NEEDS CARE

You might have come across a term called FIREWALL for computers. In simple term it is a Software Security system that prevents malicious or unauthorized traffic to enter and damage Computer system. Firewall is one such software developed to protect our computer system.

Has it ever occurred to you that our own Mind which functions like a Super Computer in resolving our complex problems could also be in need of such care and protection? Probably you have not. How can such care protection be given to our Mind? What instantly comes to our mind is giving it rest or if serious we go to a Doctor and get Medicines or just Sedatives to put it to Sleep. We actually medicate our Brains and Body to treat our Mind in a roundabout way.

It's a pity; we are deactivating a Super Computer without knowing what exactly to do. This is how we treat our Mind; just like another organ which it is not. It is an Abstract entity. !!!

An Abstract entity cannot be treated physically. It has to be treated mentally through soft commands and suggestions.

We are not used to think of our Mind in that way. In fact we hardly think much about our own mind. We generally follow whatever comes to our Mind. We never think why such thoughts come to our mind. We always think whatever comes to our Mind is our own. This is a mistake we all do. You are not same as your Mind. You should control your mind not the other way round. Hence **Disassociate yourself from your Mind.** You and your Mind are not the same. You are the Master and you can train your Mind to think the way you want it to do. The realization that your Mind can be trained the way you want it to be, is a big step forward in knowing your Mind.

Human Mind is similar to a Kaleidoscope. It presents myriads of patterns at different times. Imagine the different patterns in Kaleidoscope are like characters of different Human beings. Each Human being represents a Pattern he has opted for himself, the path that he has chosen to travel in life; his thinking process and his Lifestyle. Though the patterns in Kaleidoscope changes; the color beads, which a player manipulates to create different patterns, remain the same.

Can we arrange the Color Beads of our mind to create our own pattern? In other words can we train our Mind to achieve our Goal? The Answer is a Strong Affirmative and is the basic fabric around which this Book is woven.

CHAPTER TWO

KNOW THYSELF

"Know you" has been the Advice of Great Ancient Sages who has spent their life to arrive at this realization and have passed it on to us. And Knowing Yourself is to know your mind and is not as easy as it may sound. In fact it is quite a difficult task. If you know yourself truly, you can travel on a path of your own and face the world with confidence.

Knowing your mind is like knowing yourself. Once you know your mind, you can make it think your way, do what you want. It will be your Good Slave and not a Bad Master which so far it has been. Since we have never thought of Mind in this way, we have allowed it to rule us the way it had wanted.

What our Mind generally wants is usually based on imitating what our Friends, Peers and Society do. We do what is considered as the in thing and not what is good for us to do. We go with the winds and not knowing what to do when the direction of wind suddenly changes. We have to find out what is really good for us and what we really want in our life.

Your Mind can be trained and controlled to work for you and not against. We are in our Life what our Minds make us to be. And we in turn have to train and develop our Mind the way we want it to be during course of our lives.

It is interlinked. If we don't train and control our Mind and let it be our Master it will guide us based on prevailing circumstances and norms and without any fixed goal. We will just be tossing around back and forth in this ocean of the World at command of the waves.

A lot of books have been written and advices given by Life Style Gurus and Motivational Speakers on how to improve on your mind capabilities. The Books would cite numerous cases of how people became famous from brinks of disaster by following principles laid down in those books. Gurus would advise you to follow them and assure you that soon you would be transformed into a wonderful person. All your past failures would fade and new ventures turn into success stories and future would look bright and promising. Advices well given but rarely followed. The Advices are good and well intended. But will they act as a general panacea for all? Is one medicine good for all ailments? But if they had made their mark on all the readers, we would have by now equal number, if not more, of readers joining the Hall of Fame.

The Advisors might have made themselves rich but the most of the followers are not. Have you ever thought of that? In brief, the advices were given to follow some goals in Life. Mostly Money, Power, Fame and similar goals. But they may not be your desired goals in life. You have to discover your own Goal and then only take help from others in travelling your desired path. Nobody can dictate your Goal except you. Your trained mind will do it for you as you only know and can manipulate the beads in your Kaleidoscope and arrange them to your desired pattern. And nobody else can.

The stories you hear about successful persons tell you only half the truth, the glittering side only. What about their minds which guided them to success. You will never come to know of it. Every Human Mind is as unique as his Finger print. You can never copy and paste to produce another successful person. You can know of his struggles on his way to success but not of his inner self which propelled it to success. And there is no single yard stick of how you measure success. Your conception of success may be some one's worst dream of a Disaster.

You may also note that these advices are mostly aimed at making Money, Lots of Money as if it is a pre requisite for Peace and Salvation. Hardly anybody talks of How to be Happy. Happiness is considered a By Product of Money. Thus every human being has a different Goal to be discovered and achieved by him only.

This is beautifully illustrated by writer Hermann Hess in his Nobel wining book "Siddhartha". Siddhartha went to Lord Buddha to find out how he attended Nirvana; i.e. freedom from all worldly worries and attends a state of super consciousness. Many followers of Buddha tried their best to explain to him in so many words but failed to convince him. He went to Lord Buddha himself with his query.

Buddha told him it is not possible to explain unless you go through the same stages yourself. The story moves on and finally Siddhartha discovered his peace mind on his own in adopting a simple lifestyle of ferrying people down across River Ganges and found containment with persons around him.

The point to note here is not the Goal he reached, it could be different for each of us but the way he achieved it. It was through self analysis. Thus no matter whoever advises you, including mine, unless you're Mind accepts it, they will go waste. And your Mind will accept it only when you feel it from within. Otherwise it will go waste.

When imposed from the Top, a pursuit of Positive Goals sometimes introduces Negativity in your mind. Wanting to be stress free you become stressful. Positive advices thus strangely lead to Negative result. This is a strange phenomenon. Gurus won't take responsibility for this. Their Advices were certainly good and not to be discounted with. But sadly they fell on a mind not prepared to accept them and probably not meant for them, let alone benefit from it.

Each person has its own criteria of acceptance and his mind at different stage of development. Thus flooding your mind with countless tales of most successful persons in the world may hardly produce any result. Seeds sown on a land not prepared won't bear fruits. The land has to be made ready first. Then sow the seeds but hold on, what seeds you are going to sow??
You want lots of Money, Enormous Power to wield or Peace of Mind or maybe a nice Cocktail of all. Whatever it is, your inner mind has to accept the choice. Thus what nobody tells you is how to prepare your mind before you embark upon any program to pursue your goal. You cannot suddenly transform your mind. First you have to know what's in there.
Most likely you have the Jewel there waiting to be discovered. Instead of looking inward, may be you have been running around in circle in search of success stories. Now before you start knowing your mind, it may be good to first know what state is it presently in.

CHAPTER THREE

STATE OF OUR MIND

Let us ponder a little on our present state of Mind.

In pursuit of our livelihood we have been reduced to a state where we have no time to think about us, let alone about others. We have become so much Self Centered that we first forget people around us, and then forget our friends; relatives, our Parents and ultimately our wife and Children and finally we are left alone. Nobody is present around us but we go on clicking down on Computer Key Board with vengeance.

Obsession with Technology is another aspect which is adversely affecting our lives. We have been working like a slave for Machines, developing new devices or software for it and in the process have given our Mind a Miss. We have been also naive to believe that achieving a technical excellence will also excel our Mind and quality of our lives. Experience tells otherwise.

This is not to undermine the roll of Technological advancement. I have been a computer personal myself during my professional career and know of its importance. In fact we all know of its importance but we fail to realize that we now know more of Computers and Technology in general than our own Mind.

Here again we have sadly let Technology to be our master to rule our lives. It so happens now that Husband and Wife staying in the same house communicating with each other by WhatsApp. And this gets gradually extended to cover most of their communication to reach a point of Disconnect in Relation. Not blaming them, they are not even aware of it till they get slowly drawn down into this Vortex of Life which engulfs them.

Our concept of Life has mostly been hard work in office or business during week days, fun during weekends with vacations dotted over a few months in a year. All these we do mechanically as the in-thing to do and all the while, a subtle fear of insecurity, a fear of uncertain future runs through our Mind which you cannot express to anybody.

This is because our ship is not anchored to a solid rock. It has not found any solid anchors of its own to tie with. It is floating around based on weak and flimsy anchors of fake social status and false glitters of our friends and peers. At this stage your Mind also do not give you full support as it is not prepared to deal with such situation. Hence neither can you enjoy your good times nor do you have any plan to counteract your future uncertainties. This is where a trained Mind could have been of help and your asset.

In pursuit of earning your bread, look, what we all have reduced ourselves to. !! Is this what we wanted? Certainly not. But then how it happened? And when and where we lost our way??

When you started your life, comfortable with a job and giving your full input to it, your close ones cheering you ON and you have only Money and Comfort on your Radar. You were then like a Horse with a Blinker, Can't see anybody else, had no time for anybody, forget others, you had no time even for yourself.

You had not even given a good look at yourself. You only knew

what you like to eat, how to work and where to go for enjoyment. All these happen in the name of earning your bread, pursuit of technology, modern living style and so on. But all these factors are mere decorations on a House that is you. If you don't survive in spite of the decorations or rather because of them, then of what use they are of?? The whole show will collapse.
You had not been then aware of this X factor called Mind which can spoil all your mundane comforts unless controlled.

The same Mind which cheered you ON in your uncharted path suddenly revolted against you and brought you down. You did not know the reasons, as it was not under your control but was guided by external influences only. The external influences are like waves on a sea Shore, they toss you back and forth at their will and you have hardly any control on them. This is exactly where you lost your way. You as a Human Being deserve most importance and need utmost care and your Mind should be your Guiding Angel. Your mind determines what you are and what you will be.

Here we will get into an analysis of this X Factor called Mind to the extent possible.

Like many others, I have also suffered Deep Agony and Frustration with no respite in sight. Betrayal by close ones, uncalled for hostilities and being thrown into desperate situation with no Light at the end of the Tunnel. Have suffered them all and had my full share of miseries. It has been truly a roller coaster drive. But this has led me to dive deeper into human life and shaded areas of mind. Many suffer in this way and hold others responsible for their miseries. Finally they end up in blaming Fate or God and since none of them are within our control, it will be futile to blame them, we can only pray for a solution.

We cannot blame God or Fate for our miseries as we are not aware of how they operate but going by some common experiences, their action is not always based on logic or righteousness. Rather they sometimes exhibit a Cynical sense of Humor. Many Good people suffer most and bad are exalted. Since the secret behind their operation have yet not been fully decoded, it is better not to solely depend on them. Prepare your Mind and firmly believe in yourself. If their help comes, gratefully acknowledge it, else don't blame them.

Now let us think impartially without attributing our misfortune to external factors. Could we have done something to avoid our problems or taken some action to mitigate our sufferings? I am afraid the answer is yes. Had our Mind been properly trained, we could have avoided such sufferings in most of the cases though not all. But Mind training is not commonly heard of and much less practiced. This is the main theme of this book in which the state and complexity of Mind are revealed and discussed.

The following chapters will guide you through some critical aspects of mind and how best you can train your mind for your well being. Let us get on board but you need not tighten your seat belt. Rather be relaxed and have an open mind during our trip towards exploration of Mind.

CHAPTER FOUR

TRAIN YOUR MIND

On speaking of Mind, the Mind as we commonly know of is our Logical Mind. This guides us through all our mundane activities. But we do have a Sub Conscious Mind, hence forward mentioned as "Sub Mind", which sometimes pops out to warn us of dangers ahead. Sometimes it is at conflict with our Logical Mind and disagrees with our decision taken.

Now let us get a clear picture of our two states of mind.
Our Logical Mind is our main guiding force in all our mundane activities. From our Birth and on through our journey of life, we gather lots of experience which build up our Logical mind and guide us through. In this process, we also build up our Sub Mind which gathers all the feedback from Logical Mind.

Our Logical Mind is prone to all good and bad influences and guides us through our Life with our immediate gains in mind. During this journey of Life our Sub Mind also picks up vital information but unlike the Logical Mind it analyses them and stores them as our Knowledge Base for future guidance of our Logical Mind. External influences cannot influence it easily like they do for your Logical mind. A Sub Mind is our Conscience and not easily influenced by external factors. It also gives us an advance warning of future which we sometimes call it as our Sixth Sense.

The process of Mind training is to train your Logical Mind. Your Sub Mind also gets trained up in this process. It analyses and builds up its Knowledge base for future guidance of your Logical Mind.

Your Mind training guides your present actions and your Knowledge stored in your Sub Mind builds up your Character and Conscience. Thus you achieve the best of a state where your Logical Mind and Sub Mind are in perfect Harmony.

But in cases when they are in conflict, the result is disastrous. People lose their mental balance and are at a loss to know what to do.
Some others shut their Sub Mind totally off and do whatever pleases them to do. Anti social and criminal activities is result of such a state of mind. Both these are unacceptable situations. This is where training your Mind assumes great importance.

A Trained Sub Mind will guide your Logical Mind as an Auto Pilot on your journey of life which will then be a smooth and pleasant one. And when the final Landing comes at the end of our Life's Journey it will also be smooth, without any bumps and with joy of a Life well spent and with No Regrets.

Now let us get on board now on an exciting exploration of Mind. It is often said

"MIND IS A BAD MASTER BUT A GOOD SLAVE"

Mind Control is an age wise concept, but were considered exclusive to Sages, Elites or wise Persons. Training your mind to work for you was never on the cards. People in general, as of now also, are not fully aware of potential of Mind. Its Energy can be directed either way. As your Master, it can destroy you but as a Slave it can do wonders for you.

Training our mind sounds High Sounding and Complicated but the efforts involved are small steps and are quite simple. Once your mind is trained, you will have a good control over your Thoughts, Speech and Action. Mind training is a continuous process in small steps. It is not a monolithic block of achievement which could be labeled as a Success or failure if it does or does not work. The training comprises small steps with persistent efforts like you do for your physical exercise. The difference is, it relates to mind. When you are in this process, nobody else except you will know them. It is your specific training program to be conducted by you only at your convenient time and pace. It is a dynamic process and at any point of time you have achieve a certain grade and still on the race. There are no concepts of Failure here but only achieving certain grades of Success. You never fail but achieve a grade of Success and the training process continues.

As you go through the Mind training exercises, your mind adopts the lessons and gets ready to support you. Thus when you encounter a problem, your mind is ready to prompt you with a solution. As you go on through stages of success, your confident manners, bright eyes and radiating personality will show up and your transformation will be visible to all.

CHAPTER FIVE

MIND TRAINING EXERCISES

Here are a few Mind training exercises which can be followed at your convenience and at your own pace

Mind Exercise-1
Keep Your Mind Blank

Our Minds are many times crowded with Unproductive thoughts; Trash or Garbage. We know and feel they are trash but unable to get rid of them. They come back again and again to torment us. Thus we get burdened by our trash thoughts. They control us; affect our activities and slowly our Lives. Our Brain is no place for storing Garbage. We should be in control of what to put in there.

The first step is to keep our Mind Blank. No thoughts whatsoever. Count down from 5 to 0 and at 0 count take slowly deep breaths. Inhale and exhale slowly and don't allow any thoughts to enter your Mind.

Now No thought can penetrate your Mind. If it does give it a MENTAL THROW and throw it out. Keep your Mind Blank. If any thought comes to your mind, as it will intermittently and in waves, throw it out. It's not easy. If one thought comes, say NO to it and throw it out. The next one would come, say No again. Refuse to Think. This way Negate all thoughts that would come to your mind in waves. While doing this, imagine Blissful Cosmic waves sweeping through your Body and Mind filling them with Peace.

Finally you will reach a state when no thought occupies your mind without your consent. Fill your Mind with ZERO THOUGHT. Yes a Zero Thought Mind is a blissful mind. A State where no thoughts would worry you. You may continue this practice as an Exercise. You can continue with this exercise whenever you have time and convenience.

To start with, find some free time when you are alone, close your eyes, take slow but deep breaths and try to keep your mind absolutely Blank. Imagine cosmic waves sweeping through your mind and body. Yes thoughts will keep coming but force them out. If you can keep your mind Blank at least for Five Minutes, you have a great start. Practice this regularly and slowly you will develop the Power to keep your mind absolutely Blank for longer duration as you wish. This is will be a Great Step forward. If you practice this before going to sleep, it will induce Sound Sleep. Keeping your Mind Blank has immense benefits. It has cleared your mind of all trash thoughts and gives your Mind a Rest, it so badly deserves. And more importantly it has now room for your productive thoughts.

Once you have acquired the habit of keeping your mind Blank when you wish, you have also acquired the capability of filling it with thoughts of your choice.

This Art of filling your mind with your selected thoughts or keeping it Blank at your will is a great achievement. It needs constant practice but is achievable. You will also come to realize that it is of great benefit before an Important Event or Meeting. It calms your mind and fills it up with extra energy to concentrate on your upcoming event.

Mind Exercise-2
Split Problems:

Sometimes problems are multiple, unrelated and complicated. Combined, it looks like a big Monolithic mass not amenable to solution. This looks formidable and your mind gets stressed and unable to think of any action. The way out is to split them into separate compartments, and tackle each according to its type and magnitude.

Apply a cool mind to seek a solution and take prompt action instead getting into a Mental Paralysis which occurs quite often in such cases.

Please take up the split problems one at a time. Analyze the worst case scenario for each one before deciding on course of action.

Please remember, No problem is so great that it defies a solution. Our Fear psychosis gives it a false magnitude and pumps it up as a Big Balloon. A sharp prick with your smart mind will burst this balloon.

Instead of multiple problems, sometimes you have one really big problem or assignment which looks formidable at first sight and seems no easy way out for a solution. In this case also, Split the problem into several steps and start climbing the first step of its Ladder. While climbing the first step of a ladder you don't count how many steps the ladder has but concentrate on the first step only. When the First Step has been completed get into the second one and count this as the First step and give it all importance of the first step until all the steps are covered

In this exercise, you are training your mind to concentrate on problems like you do when you concentrate sunlight on a piece of paper. When the concentration of light is high, it burns the paper. Same way it will be easier for you to concentrate your thought on a single problem the problem will burn up and disappear under your concentration.

Mind Exercise-3
Think You Are in Control:

In short terms, as a Victim your options are Limited but as a Master your Options are many.

An important thing that you must practice in your mind before you come across any problem is to feel that you are in Control of the situation **even if you are not**. You may be a victim of circumstances but think that you can still control the situation. This will immensely boost your self confidence and you will find new ways to control the situation. There are always ways to get out of a difficult situation seemingly looking Impossible.

When you think that you can still control the situation, your confidence will be high and your mind will be free from depressing effect of suffering as a Victim this is because when you look from the angle of a victim, your mind gets paralyzed, your choices get limited and they seem to lie mostly with the oppressor. But when you look from the angle of controlling the situation your options open up and mind comes up with new ways to control it.

Mind Exercise-4
Avoid Knee Jerk Reaction

Quite often, in hostile situations, such as in case of a verbal assault or a sudden provocation, we often suffer from knee jerk reaction and give out a quick response without application of our mind. This does more harm than good to us later and has to be avoided.

The best way will be to first absorb in a cool mind all that is being directed to you, then take a few seconds more to frame a suitable reply. You need some time to absorb and analyze opponent's view or the subject matter, and only then can you give out a suitable response.

This, you will find, is an excellent idea to adopt and can apply in any serious meeting or discussion. It works out Fine.

Mind Exercises-5
Extend Boundaries of Mind

People love to draw boundaries of their own. The smaller is your Boundary; more contended you are but only as long as you remain within your small world. The moment you are outside your boundary, you come across many unknown factors or things not of your choice and this will affect your peace of mind.

We now live in a world which is not only Black and White but comprises many colors and hues in between. We have to live with people of diverse characters, divergent views and have to work with them instead of being Judgmental or shutting them out of our boundary. Our Small boundaries, drawn up by us, will ensure our peace but within a small frame and for a limited period. The moment you step out of your small island that you have created for yourself, you will walk into trouble and loss of mental peace. We all know of many tribes in small islands, dotted across the Oceans living happily, cut off from the world. We cannot equate with them in this modern world of ours nor can we emulate their life style.

When we extend our mental boundaries, the problems no longer remain unknown; we either solve them or learn to live with them. They will no longer disturb peace of our mind. We no longer are in fear of unknown. Hence wider is your boundary and broader s your vision, the less will be your cause for worries.

Extending boundary broadens your mind. As you broaden your mind, flexibility of your mind increases. You are no longer bound by extremes of Right or Wrong; but learn to accept many colors of different hue in between. This does not mean that we accept and imitate others life style. Certainly not; we are only recognizing their right to live their life their own way and not draw any line in between.

With this understanding you have removed a major cause for your mental strain. A lot of problems in this world today would vanish if people adopt this philosophy in life. We have been creating more boundaries, in fact slashing small boundary into smaller ones. Sadly now we see this divisive tendency taking grip over many countries. Great civilization who once proclaimed that the whole world is One Family is falling into this trap for narrow political gains.

The Life in this World started with cells multiplying into new cells and completing a living form, but now we are in the reverse process of dividing an entire Human race into smaller segments till they reach a form of insignificance. When will this simple truth dawn on us and save us from an impending catastrophe?

Mind Exercise-6
View from Top

While in the topic of broadening one's mind there is another way of looking at your life with an impartial view.

It can be termed as a "View from the Top". View your Life from the Top, as if you are viewing your life from the Sky above as if you are not yourself but an impartial Observer.

This will disassociate yourself from you and you look at your life from Top like a stranger as if things are happening to somebody else and not to you. You are now an impartial observer. Take an impartial view of things happening to your life. Get a clear, unbiased picture of yourself and your life. You will discover many strange things about yourself hitherto unknown. And this could be your Best Guidance for future.

When viewed from top, a forest looks beautiful, but when you go down to trees, the view gets complicated, distorted and confusing. A Macro level view of Life, that is how you want your Life to be, should shape your Micro level activities and not the other way round.

Mind Exercise-7
Read other's Mind

Types of Mind training exercises are many and its application varied in nature. A trained mind should read others mind as well. Many times when we talk to people, the discussion seems cordial and fruitful. Many things are promised and assured but it so happens that the result does not match with our expectation and

quite often it is disappointing. It happens with all of us.
Have you ever thought of why it happens like this??

The key to this question is again Mind. Your opponent's Mind. You know yours but have not studied well his mind. When we interact with a person during friendship, love or any other reason; our interaction level stays confined to verbal exchanges. Eye contacts and body languages are not given much importance. We draw our conclusions mostly based on verbal exchanges. But this is not enough. Let's get a little deeper.

A valuable technique to be acquired is how to read others mind from looking straight at their eyes, reading brow movements and body languages. A lot have been written on the subject and is good to go through them.

In situations such as Relations, Love, Friendship our first reaction is to fall back on our Sub Mind; Our gut feelings. In this case our Logical Mind is usually not activated. We get swept away by our first feeling and not look at it logically. Get out of Mist that is clouding your logical thoughts and apply your logics. It may sound a lot Unromantic but a stable relation is lot better than a broken heart.

On the other hand, in situations such as any business or similar mundane dealings, we use our Logical Mind first. We usually do not fall back on our Sub Mind which could have given us a gut feeling.

In both the above cases, our responses need a course correction. Thus during Flight of your Life, unlike normal flights, take the help of both Normal and Autopilot modes simultaneously.

But before doing all these, first root your mind to the present and focus on the subject. If your mind wanders off the situation, the valuable inputs will be lost.

Exercise-8
Root Your Mind To Present:

Many times when we are dealing with a problem or situation or say even in a meeting, our mind wanders off. We start thinking about past or future events not connected with the present situation. Sometimes it happens even when we are on road or travelling. Many times it results in loss of valuable articles and even in accidents.

Rooting your mind to the present means think actively and note details of happenings and people around you while you are carrying out some activity. You may be out on a business, a meeting or on tours or holidays; it would be good to study people and happenings around you. It does not mean you have to on guard all the time and strain yourself. This should be a natural state of mind.

As a part of rooting your mind exercise, remember to take "One Minute Pause" before any action or event. Before you leave our house for a meeting or any other event it is good to take a pause for one minute, root yourself to the present situation and take a count on essential things or document you may be leaving behind.

Similarly before leaving a meeting or a place of visit, pause for a minute and think of what could not be discussed or any action not taken. Such routine one minute pause saves you lots of trouble later.

To sum up, please focus your mind to the present while dealing with a situation or activity. You can practice the luxury of wandering mind when you have free time for it.

Exercise-9
Face the Problem Headway:

Fear of facing a Problem makes us delay it and this does not help in its solution. When a problem confronts you, most of the time it deserves an immediate attention. We delay it for fear of confrontation and avoid meeting it face to face. This does not solve the problem but rather aggravates it. Shake the fear out, take that phone call or meet that person face to face and most of the time the problems get solved.

Of course in some rare cases, where delay is to your advantage, you can go for it. But such cases are few and require your careful discretion.

Exercise-10
COMPASSION IN JUDGEMENT

We have now completed most our Mind Training exercises and well prepared to face the world head on. Our mind is a weapon now but should never be used in general as such. It should not make us take an offensive position because of our training. A defensive attitude and a compassionate nature should be the right Mindset.

Ego should not creep in following your improved Mindset. Ego is the harmful Byproduct for most achievement. Many successful persons suffer from this malady. When you achieve success in one narrow field, you think you know everything, all aspects of Life and belittle everyone else. A mind full of Ego is like shutting your windows to the world and creating an island of your own where you perceive yourself to be the Monarch of all you survey. Please avoid this dreadful trap.

It is said that we are our Best Lawyer but Worst Judge for others. This is True to a large extent. When we judge others for a simple failing or a mistake on their part, we do it in haste and in a harsh manner without any compassion in our mind.

But when we are judged, we expect lots of understanding and compassion. A strange situation but happens too often. A little application of mind with logical thinking would have corrected the situation. Thus a little bit of compassion and understanding on our part will multiply several folds and come back to us from others as our reward.

As you mind gets slowly trained this way, you will realize that you have trained a Giant **GENIE** of enormous power to obey your command, which is none other than your Mind, to be at your Service always. It will not only obey all your commands as and when you issue them but the Sub Mind will prompt you automatically for your course correction if required. The process is simple and does not involve any rigorous practices or strenuous efforts. And a big take away is there is no chance of Failures, No sense of defeat or loss of face before your Friends. This a silent work to be carried out in steps by you at your own pace and convenience.

CHAPTER SIX

FREE YOURSELF FROM CHAINS OF YOUR OWN CREATION:

As Rousseau once said " **Man is born free but every where he is in chains".** Would like to add a little suffix

Here as

"And this chain is mostly created by man himself".

Hence a Mind without any chains or constraints is truly a Free Mind and is capable for higher stages of development. Such a mental stage enables you to think clearly and set your target accurately.

Another chain that we usually create for ourselves is dependence on prediction of Astrologers. In predicting your Future, they ruin your present. They gain their Fees and you lose your Confidence you are looser both ways; your money and your confidence. If predictions are Firm and you can never alter them. Then why go for it in advance?

The story has it that Babur; the founder of Mughal Empire in India had to face a strange problem during his early days of rule.
Lots of complain came to him from his people that Indian Astrologers were predicting evil things about future thus upsetting their mental condition.

The King ordered them to invite the Best Astrologer in India to his court. Accordingly the Best Astrologer of that time was presented in the court. The King asked the Astrologer to predict Day and Time of his own Death and how would he die. The Astrologer Predicted that he would die after a certain years suffering from some disease. The King asked him to recheck it. The Astrologer confirmed his prediction. At this point The King took out his sword and beheaded him instantly. The King had thus sent out a strong message to his people and after that the fear of astrological predictions was gone forever.

Is it not strange that the astrologers predict and maintain that their prediction are invincible but at the same time they prescribe some articles such as rings and other wearable which can ward of the impending disaster.

They are earning both ways but people fail to see that and fall for them. The belief that some distant Stars, light years away would guide our future rather than our own actions is hard to comprehend.

Obviously, it is the fear of Unknown which forces people in this direction. Your Future can be shaped by only your own Action and not by appeasement of any external forces through astrologers. Distant stars light years away cannot shape your future. Any unknown incidents predicted in future do not call for straining your mind right now. Your strong mind will take care of it when it actually happens.

Apart from dependence on astrological predictions, we also bind ourselves with certain inhibitions and prejudices which restrain us from taking logical decisions. It is like, as mentioned earlier, we bind ourselves with chains of our own creation. Prejudices sap our energy, and cripple our ability to counter a problem when required and then we blame fate for any mishaps resulting out of it. This is like tying our own hands and feet and then trying to swim. Any adverse outcome of this situation is the result of our own action. But we usually put the blame on wrong things such as bad timings, wrong position of some distant Stars, color of dresses we wear, or the first face we saw when we got out of our bed in the morning.

Talking of Inhibitions which turns slowly to Belief, Some spend lots of time and effort in consulting some experts while building a house. These Experts will speak volumes on which direction to locate your House and different rooms to get good effects from distant stars rather than basing their advices on Meteorological, Environmental, Earthquake or Tsunami consideration.

It is ironical to note that all our location and directions such as East/West or North/South constantly change with respect to the distant stars or heavenly bodies due to rotation of our planet Earth as well as of theirs !!!. Then how wills a specific direction in Earth will be of any benefit from heavenly bodies? And as regards any direction specific to Earth, Meteorological and Environmental consideration should have been the prime consideration in this case but are not considered that way.

However since Belief is not a scientific Phenomenon, advices against it would not be proper and at best futile. The sooner we realize this and free ourselves from these prejudices, the better for our lives. We will then truly be free from any chains of our own creations.

CHAPTER SEVEN

STAY REAL, NOT VIRTUAL

We all feel and suffer from the stress and strain induced by our present style of living; the modern civilization as we say. The modern civilization is our creation, a process of evolution over million years have put us where we are now. We reap its benefits but not prepared to bear its fall out of sufferings and strains.

Instead of facing the problems headway, we sometime try to bypass it on some pretext. The fear to face the real world and a tendency to bypass it, is probably leading us to creation of a Virtual world where things will be as we wish them to be. This is like hiding inside a cocoon and getting slowly isolated from the real world. This feeling is now real and widespread. This fear and aversion to react with real world has probably led to creation of an artificial new 3D universe.

This is now real and happening. Now there is a virtual 3D world where you can interact virtually with people, go on a virtual holiday and practically do everything that you do in Real world. In this artificial world you can even be represented by your Avatars, not your real self. Further Isolation!!!

In the name of Advancement of Technology, Human beings and Human qualities are being pushed to the back. Technology is advancing at the cost of Humanity. People are being replaced by their Avatars.

This new concept of Virtual Universe will slowly engulf us and ruin our personal lives. When you feel like crying you will not a get a real shoulder to fall back upon. You have to Cry Virtually.

In a Virtual World, interpersonal dealing will decrease leading to further isolation. Creating Cocoons as a safe dwelling place.

In one life you never gather all the precious stones that the Life has to offer. People work together, exchange knowledge and experience and that's how the Civilization advances and Human values and Experiences are carried forward leading to progress of Science and Technology. All this requires a constant interaction with fellow human beings and virtual concept and life style will be detrimental to this.

Apart from ill effects of virtual world concept, heavy influx of technology without proper control will also poses a great warning sign in our lives.

The aim of new technology is supposed to be for improvement of human lives. But now it has been an unholy competition between super powers on how to convert them to weapons of mass destruction.

Hence it is for us to determine whether we surrender meekly to advanced technology or control and improve it with reins in our hand.

If you broadly look at some of the major developments such as Artificial Intelligence (AI) and Brain Computer Interface (BCI); both are expanding without any ethical restraint.

In one type of development; Technology is slowly controlling our Minds and our Lives such as Artificial Intelligence; Mind you, it is not "All Intelligence" which they proclaim. You may argue here that the AI Program is a Human development. True, human logic is given as Input to develop such software but at some point when human logic is not available to cover all possibilities, extrapolation and arbitrary extension of logic is adopted which may not be right, to say the least but could be also harmful.

This has actually happened with some generative AI software which has misled its users. More serious damages could happen in future.

Further the Human Logic changes over a period of time based on Socio Economic conditions and these changes are less likely to be introduced later to the AI software already developed. The people in general have hardly any say on AI software development and much less on its modification. They will continue to it blindly and suffer from its negative consequences.

Another tendency which is slowly coming up is to label everything as an AI product. You will soon find common appliances such as TV, Radio, and Kitchen appliances will all be labeled as AI product and marketed with higher prices. You cannot be sure about operational convenience of these products as you know how a smart TV takes more time to be ON than a good old TV. But one thing you can be sure, these products will require less and less use of your original gray matter but use more and more of Artificial matter.

The other type ofimportant developmentis Brain Computer Interface (BCI) where it is other way round. The Mind here is controlling the Machine. A fantastic development indeed if it is used as is being contemplated now. This will enable physically impaired persons to see, hear and control their movements. If the Brain Implants are too invasive, it may raise Ethical consideration against it. Also when transmission capability of the Implants increases sufficiently, it may be possible to read others mind as well. But will that be good and acceptable?

We can only ensure through our collective opinion that their applications should be strictly controlled. The world had been witness to its devastating effects of Technology many times. But the Technology as it exists today is far more potent and can be far more devastating than anything that existed till date. Till date it had the capability to destroy the Human race but now it has more devastating effect; it can now modify the entire Human race.

It is our decision now. We are Humans and it is our world and the only one such in the Universe to our knowledge.

CHAPTER EIGHT

EXPLORE THE FOUNTAIN OF HAPPINESS WITHIN; YOUR OWN ARTISAN WELL

We have talked about protecting our Mind against harmful influences affecting peace of our mind through building a Firewall. We have also talked about freeing ourselves from self defeating Inhibitions and Prejudices. Now our Mind has turned into a blissful, protected place free of any inhibitions.

Absence of Disturbance however is not synonym with Peace or Happiness but your mind now is a ground well prepared to sow seeds of Peace and Happiness. How do we do that? We first have to define and set our own version of Peace and Happiness.

Peace and Happiness are our natural state of Mind. We should enjoy Peace and Happiness as we enjoy God gifted Ones like Air, Water and Sunshine. They should naturally be with us but we miss them too often due to our distorted view of Life and concept of Happiness.

True as a part of earning our livelihood we run after Money, as our immediate goal and indulge in power game and social status as necessary evils but do they give us happiness and peace of mind? They provide us comfort and pleasure but with lots of strains and worries. But not true happiness or peace of mind. And when you fall where is your Safety Net? There will be none unless you have build up one within you slowly over years. Hence look for support within. Your trained mind will be your solid anchor during your bad days and a source of happiness forever.

Peace of Mind should come from a Fountain of Happiness embedded in our Mind such as an Artisan Well inside us. Artisan wells are found in some parts of Australia and also in some other parts of the world where water spontaneously flows out of the well like a spring. Peace and Happiness should flow out of our Mind as an Artisan well. But the Mud and Silt deposit created by us chokes the mouth of this well stopping its natural flow. We cannot blame any external factors for this but we with our distorted view of Life and Happiness are responsible for this state of Mind.

This brings us to the topic of defining our view of Life and Happiness.

Clear and Simple thinking is our natural habit. We are born with it but as we grow older, multiple choices make it difficult for us. Our choice for making a decision no more depends on whether a choice is good or bad for us but whether it will be useful for us to scale higher ladders of Social status or it will result in any immediate or future gains for us.

An important aspect of our life today is tremendous influence wielded by social, print and visual media in our lives. Our aspirations get guided by them. Many of our Goals are set by Social Media. Posts of some of your friends holidaying in some Tourist

Paradise or someone presenting his wife with some expensive jewelry or a Car or someone dining in expensive restaurants influences your mind. All these may trigger yours or your wife's ambition and that may set a goal in your mind.

We thus fix our goals just to compete with our friends or neighbors. This induces you to fix a goal in your life which your inner self may reject later

What actually happens is we get guided by contemporary action taken by our friends or peers who again are influenced by social media. We float in the waves and get tossed back and forth in multiple directions. We have no time to think whether it is good for us. The choice however is not as simple as choosing between good or bad. It is a strange mixture of some good and may be more of bad. We deliberately choose some evil for our immediate gains or advancement in our Social or Professional status. In this case, how would any advice benefit you? A medicine wrongly applied and that too knowingly cannot be expected to produce any result.

Another factor which clouds your selection of Goal is your hangover with your Past events or worry about the future.

Past failures are split milk. You cannot retrieve the milk but only learn how not to split again. Future is not a clear vision but only an imaginary view created by you when looking through your frosted glasses. You create an image of your own which either frightens you or elevates you on a false pedestal of Happiness. It is the present that needs more attention and more inward thinking as only this will shape our Future.

Another factor which sometimes influences us is a few religious or political persons who are flush with money or wielding enormous Power. We start idealizing them and look at them as a fittest and most successful person. But be careful with your choice in this regard.

Survival of Fittest, now a day, does not necessarily relate to most competent person. They are often not the person with most abilities, good qualities or more human values. Rather, they are often the most cunning, conniving and scheming person who climb up easily the Corporate or Business ladder.

An analogy can be drawn to Jelly Fishes who have No Brains, No Heart and No Vertebra and yet are the longest survivors in this Earth and some of their species are said to be Immortal. But the Analogy may be a little unfair to the Jelly Fishes who really have No Brains. But persons with such special abilities do have Brains but no vertebra and no Heart and they use this lethal combination to best of their advantage. However such persons are quite often idealized by our present society and held in high esteem.

Thus when we get influenced by these considerations, we frost our own looking glass and looking through this we decide our future course of action. When your looking glass is frosted and stained, it generates trashes in name of happiness and chokes the flow of your Artisan well. With all these Consideration in your trained Mind, you are now ready and careful to set your own Goal. To fix up your Goal honestly you may also have to indulge in an internal debate within yourself and then arrive at your goal. This could be anything you choose but you only will be responsible for your Choice.

Once a goal is fixed and choice of path selected, your action gets guided by this choice and your mind accepts this as your identity. A silent Command goes out to your Sub Mind where it gets embedded. This builds your Autopilot mode. Now you are relieved of thinking every time before taking a decision. Your subconscious mind will guide you on correct path and will and will warn you when you deviate from your chosen path.

During our journey in course of Life, we sometimes deliberately ignore these warning signals and the results are not enviable. We bring in unnecessary strains in to our life with no solutions in sight.

You think well, you do a good work and peace and wellness will spring out of you like an Artisan Well.
Your trained Sub Mind will be the force behind your Artisan Well.

While doing a good work or helping somebody, a feeling of ego creeps into our mind. Beware of this. A good work done benefits us as much as it benefits the subject. It elevates our spirits, creates our own Artisan Well and builds up our own peace of mind.

It sometimes happens that a person, for whom you have done some good, goes against you. It is a part of Human nature, accept it but never spoil your peace of mind. Never spoil your Artisan Well, the well where your peace and well-being springs out in continuous stream. It is never to be hurt, whatever may be the cause.

CHAPTER NINE

BUILD UP A FIREWALL FOR YOUR MIND

A Firewall for Mind, as you know by now is a Computer Security System that protects your computer from malicious attack or unwanted traffic.

Exactly the same happens with your mind and it needs protection from bad incidents or vicious attacks by your enemies. Sometimes such incidents look formidable as if the whole World is coming to an end for you. In reality they are not what they look like. They only appear so to our weak mind. Our Friends and Neighbors sometimes contribute to it and build it up to a large magnitude. But In most of the cases, they are manageable and turn out to be simple whimpers.

You are also attacked from within your mind with Negative, Unproductive and Depressing thoughts. They are sometimes more serious as they are not so apparent and visible. They destroy a person from within and sap all his energy like a termite slowly eating into valuables.

Hence you need to build up a Firewall for your Mind to protect your Mind from such onslaughts. This Firewall will put barriers to protect your mind and will be in a position to put you in

Commanding position of any problem encountered by you.

This Firewall will also build up a well of happiness within you.

How do you build up such a Firewall for Mind?

Now that you have all the components with you to build up such a Firewall for your Mind, the task should be easy.

You now know what is in your Mind, the state it is in and now it is free from most inhibitions. Most importantly you are now in practice of all Mind exercises. Your Mind is now set for installation of your Firewall.

It will be now be a process of giving soft commands to your Mind based on your realization of its state and Mind exercises that you have practiced. Once you slowly train and command your Mind this way, you will gradually realize that your Mind has already built up a Firewall for you.

From a different perspective, your trained Mind has transformed itself to be your Firewall.

It is now stable with a solid anchor to defend you against external as well as internal onslaughts. You are no longer at the whims of anybody in this world but master of your own. You have now the courage to stand against the wind when it does not blow your way.

Think nothing can end my world. Just chant it in your mind

"Nothing can upset me"
"I don't care" and
"I will be the Master of any Situation".

Your trained Mind, your Firewall will also open up a well of happiness within you.

40

CHAPTER TEN

EARTH WATER FIRE

It's not a good idea to harbor hatred against your enemy. Hatred harms you more than your enemy. Take action but don't keep garbage like Hatred in your sacred place called Mind.

In this present world of ours, we are being constantly subjected to unfair actions, malicious treatment from others. We can't let it go. We know we have to act against injustice. Act then, but never harbor Hatred in your mind. Your mind is an abode of Peace and not a place to store Garbage.

Your mind is now protected by your Own Firewall which protects it against External Threats as well as internal ones. Your Artisan well springs out Peace and Happiness for you and maintains this blissful situation and never let it go. Please remember and chat three things in your mind.

EARTH WATER FIRE

Build up Tolerance power like Earth. It coolly accepts many abuses of humankind. Water is cool. Be cool like Water. Your mind should race like Fire. It should be Fast, Cool and Active like Fire. These are good things to remember and act upon.
Lop sided development in Technology without any Human values or advancement in Human life quality will spell disaster for

Humanity.

There are many big countries in the world today that have the Best Technology and are the Economic Power houses but lag far behind in offering Quality of Life. Many small Nordic countries are in the Forefront in this regard. They offer the best quality in living style and contentment but are far behind in GDP or Technological Superiority.

The same happens with an individual also and in his life he has to make this delicate choice. All that we have discussed so far are expected to make your choice easier. The Book does not prompt you to accept a particular choice but offers you a tool for making the right choice. It is your Life and the choice entirely yours. It is a learning process and you learn and improve from your mistakes. Never mind your mistakes and never cow down before adverse situation. Remember Nothing in the World deserve so much Importance and least your problems.

No problem is permanent in this Temporary World. Size the Problem correctly, address it properly and get rid of it as soon as you can. Why carry it like a burden on you like Hercules carrying the globe. Care for Good things in Life which are truly free, such as Love, Affection, Friendship and Beauties of Nature like Air, Water, Flowers and Sunshine. This will increase Richness and Quality of your mind and boost your Artisan Well. And lastly please remember the Key Words are:

MINDCONTROL, FIREWALL, ARTISAN WELL.